The Motherless New Mother's Pregnancy Journal

The Motherless New Mother's Pregnancy Journal

PROMPTS, PRACTICES, AND AFFIRMATIONS
TO GUIDE THE MOM WHO IS MISSING HER OWN

Melissa Pennel

FOLLOW YOUR FIRE PUBLISHING

Melissa Pennel / Follow Your Fire Publishing FollowYourFireCoaching.com
Sacramento, CA.

Ordering Information:
Quantity sales: Special discounts are available on quantity purchases by corporations, associations, and others. For details, contact the publisher at the address above.

The Motherless New Mother's Pregnancy Journal — Prompts, Practices, and Affirmations to Guide the Mom Who is Missing Her Own — 1st ed.

Paperback ISBN: 978-1-956446-13-5
Hardcover ISBN: 978-1-956446-14-2

This journal belongs to ....

I am the daughter of ....
(MOTHER'S NAME)

She is the daughter of ....
(MATERNAL GRANDMOTHER)

My due date is ....

I am the mother of ....
(MY NEW CHILD'S NAME)

May this journal symbolize the
unbroken connection of love we share

~ For the new moms ~
May you feel supported, guided,
and reminded that you are not alone on this journey

Contents

A Note to the New Mother

Congratulations, dear new mama. You are embarking on such an incredible journey and I'm so glad you've chosen this journal to accompany you.

The practices within it will spark reflection, guide you to an inner knowing, and create a space to connect with both your new baby and your mom. The journal was created with the knowledge that becoming a mother while missing your own is a uniquely challenging, connective, and transformative experience: all things I learned on my own journey.

When my mom died in my late twenties, I had no idea how I could get through a day without her, let alone become a mom myself. Who would I call for the kind of help I saw was needed in parenting? Who would hold the baby so that I could sleep, reassure me when I felt anxious, and answer my late night phone calls about feeding, sleeping, and things I didn't yet even know to worry about? Who would celebrate milestones, welcome a deluge of baby pictures, and relish the details of not just the big things, but the small and insignificant moments too?

In the early days of grief, I couldn't picture becoming a mother because I was just trying to put one foot in front of the other. But as the raw pain of early loss changed shape, it began to coexist with beauty found in a life that somehow *did* manage to go on. The loss of our mothers can leave a wound that feels like it will never mend, but as our hearts continue to beat and new experiences join old memories, our motherless selves grow vines of strength around our grief.

And – if we're so lucky – these bodies that already house so much can also carry new life. As that new life grows within you, I want to share the most important thing I've learned on my own path: *our mothers are not absent from our mothering journey, no matter how long they've been gone.* Your mom is here, right now, at the very moment you read these words. She lives on in you, and is poured into your very foundation: an influence that might not always show, but whose presence loved the "structure" of you into being.

Our moms are still here because they live within every part of us, and I offer this journal as a way to conjure that power during a precious part of your life. Let these pages calm you mentally, nurture you spiritually, and anchor you at a time that can feel exciting yet uncertain. And as you dive in, please remember that this is a sensitive time where professional support can be helpful too. See the appendix on page 129 for information on finding professional mental health resources in your area. Also consider joining the group "Motherless Mothers: Pregnancy and Postpartum Support" on Facebook. There you'll find a growing community of other motherless pregnant and postpartum moms who are supporting one another. You don't have to travel this road alone and it's okay to ask for additional support.

May these pages be a respite and balm. May they remind you that you already have everything you need to be a wonderful mother. May they nurture the faith, hope, and love that connects you to every mother everywhere, and especially to your own, forever.

With Love,
Melissa Pennel

Suggestions, Rituals & Ideas

Treat this journaling space as a special portal — a unique way to thread connection between your higher self, your mom, and your new baby. The following pages contain ideas for how to do that.

Suggestions, Rituals & Ideas

There is no right or wrong way to approach this journaling space or these questions. You might start it on day one of pregnancy and journal chronologically, or you might pick it up in the third trimester and skip around, seeing what feels resonant. The only rule is that you give yourself permission to answer honestly, imperfectly, and allow whatever comes through you on that day to be enough. Consider this journal a practice in remembering that your best is always enough (an important lesson for motherhood *and* life.)

It can be helpful to create a ritual around the writing you do here: a series of practices that set the tone for how you want to treat this sacred space. These practices are a way to build connection with your inner guide, attune to the still-present love and guidance from your mom, and deepen the connection you are forging with your new baby. This journal also creates a space to connect with your own Higher Power, a term you can use interchangeably with whatever language feels most comfortable for you.

What follows are some suggestions on how to approach the writing you do here. Feel free to take what works, leave what doesn't, and get creative.

RITUALS
When sitting down to write, close your eyes and attune to your breath. Consider that this breath has never failed you, always been with you, and is now nourishing your growing child. Recall that this

same breath has continued since the moment you were placed into your own mom's arms when you were a baby. Observe it going in and out, feel it expand and relax your belly, and see how it connects you to both your ancestors and your child. Breathe at your own pace for as long as it feels nourishing, and allow that breath to form a sacred space as you begin to write.

• • •

Keep a candle nearby. When writing in the journal, light the candle and take a few moments to watch the flame dance. Set an intention, and then allow the light to keep vigil with you as you write within these pages. When you're done writing, whisper a "thank you" and blow the candle out.

• • •

Find a picture of your mom and tuck it within the journal. Before sitting down to write, pull out the picture and study it. Notice the familiar curve of her mouth, eyes, and face - remember how it felt to be in her presence and in actual conversation. Ask her to join you as you write, and envision her sitting beside you, over your shoulder, watching your hand move across the page. Relax into the easy familiarity you had with your mom, and allow it to take the pressure off of writing "well" or "right." (This ritual is especially helpful for the prompts designed to consider how your mom might have advised you around a specific issue.)

• • •

Gather sacred objects to join you at your writing space. Maybe it's a crystal that has always felt magical, an ultrasound picture of your child, a ring that your mom loved, and a pair of yet-to-be-filled baby shoes. You might burn some sweet-smelling oil, soften the lighting, and make any physical changes to your environment that signal to your body and spirit that this is a sacred time.

• • •

When finished writing, draw a bath, take a walk, or put on some comforting music. It's a tender and brave thing to journal truthfully, and it's important that you tend to yourself as you walk this path. Just as your mom cared for you when you were young, and just as you're going to tend and nourish the child you're growing, regard yourself as deserving of love, attention, and care. Practice treating yourself with the love you need now and always.

• • •

Treat this journal as a sacred space — Let whatever flows through you be exactly right and always good enough. Remind yourself that you are too.

Breathe in, breathe out, repeat.

Onward.

The First Trimester

The first trimester of pregnancy brings up a lot. Finding out the big news is often a moment of both joy and terror, excitement and uncertainty — confusing reactions for any new mother, but especially the motherless mother. You might feel especially in need of your own mom's wisdom as this time likely finds you both excited and untethered. As your waist begins to expand your deep vulnerability does too; your organs will rearrange and so will your ideas of yourself, the world, and your connection to your ancestors.

Like many moments in motherhood, this early time is a beautiful mix of difficulty and beauty; deep grief and unbridled joy. Use the prompts on the following pages to reflect on important practical questions for this trimester, pose sweet and fun considerations around your growing baby, and also plumb the deep emotional and spiritual depths that this new life is inviting.

It's a lot to hold, dear new mother, but you are deeply capable of holding it all. Allow these reflections to guide you on this path.

First Trimester Reflections

Why I wanted to become a parent: ....
....
....
....
....
....
....
....
....

My conception journey in a few sentences: ....
....
....
....
....
....
....
....

The moment I found out I was pregnant: ....
....
....
....
....
....
....

How I told my partner: ....

....

....

....

....

....

....

....

The first signs of pregnancy: ....

....

....

....

....

....

....

....

Some recent emotional ups and downs: ....

....

....

....

....

....

....

WEEK

Symptoms I am feeling: ....
....
....
....
....
....
....
....

WEEK

Symptoms I am feeling: ....
....
....
....
....
....
....
....

WEEK

Symptoms I am feeling: ....
....
....
....
....
....
....

WEEK

Things I am craving: ....
....
....
....
....
....
....

WEEK

Things I am craving: ....
....
....
....
....
....
....
....
....

WEEK

Things I am craving: ....
....
....
....
....
....

I'm grateful to my body because: ....

WEEK ....

....

....

....

....

....

....

....

....

I'm grateful to my body because: ....

WEEK ....

....

....

....

....

....

....

....

....

I'm grateful to my body because: ....

WEEK ....

....

....

....

....

....

....

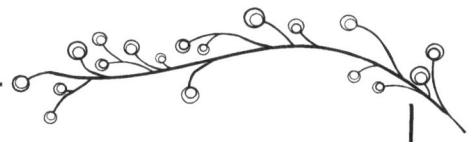

What I've learned as I research my local birth options (hospital policies, my insurance options, local birth centers, at-home midwifery care, doula recommendations, costs involved with each, etc.):

....

....

....

....

....

....

....

....

....

....

....

....

....

....

....

....

....

....

....

....

....

....

....

....

....

I am feeling nervous about: ....
....
....
....
....
....
....
....
....

Things I am looking forward to: ....
....
....
....
....
....
....
....
....

Things I am changing (or becoming conscious of) in order to have a healthy pregnancy: ....
....
....
....
....
....
....

Resources I have found especially helpful (books, podcasts, classes, teachers, etc.):

....

....

....

....

....

....

....

....

Qualities I want my care team to possess (calming, skilled, gentle, kind, experienced, etc.): ....

....

....

....

....

....

....

....

How I want to feel about my birthing care team (supported, safe, trusting, etc.):

....

....

....

....

....

....

....

My intentions for pregnancy (feelings such as healthy, peaceful, trusting, safe, hopeful, supported, etc.):

Who to Share the News With

It's commonly suggested to keep pregnancy news private until the end of the first twelve weeks because this time can be so tentative and tender. This advice is founded in protecting a new mother from having to share any unexpected news with a "too-wide" circle of people, but keeping the news private also means that you don't have important support during what can be an exhausting time. This is especially true for the motherless mother.

In order to honor this unique position and garner the support your mother might have provided, it can be helpful to share the news with people you choose with thoughtful intention and consideration. Take some space to consider who to share the news with below.

Who in my life do I find is uniquely supportive, nourishing, and trustworthy?

....

....

....

....

....

....

....

....

....

....

....

....

Write to Mom:

Ways you inspired me to become a mom:

....

....

....

....

....

....

....

....

....

....

....

....

....

....

....

....

....

....

....

....

....

....

....

....

What I know about your pregnancy and birth story with me/my sibling(s):

....
....
....
....
....
....
....
....
....
....
....
....
....
....
....
....
....
....
....
....
....
....

What I think you would say about my pregnancy:

Moments I have especially missed you in this first trimester:

Messages to Mom: ....
....
....
....
....
....
....
....
....
....
....
....
....
....
....
....
....
....
....
....
....
....
....
....
....
....
....
....
....

Write to Baby

WEEK .... YOU ARE CURRENTLY THE SIZE OF ....

Some memorable moments from this week: ....

....

....

....

....

....

WEEK .... YOU ARE CURRENTLY THE SIZE OF ....

Some memorable moments from this week: ....

....

....

....

....

....

WEEK .... YOU ARE CURRENTLY THE SIZE OF ....

Some memorable moments from this week: ....

....

....

....

....

....

....

When I found out I was pregnant with you I felt: ....
....
....
....
....
....
....
....
....
....
....
....
....
....
....
....
....
....
....
....
....
....
....
....
....

The first signs you sent me (physical, emotional, spiritual):

....

....

....

....

....

....

....

....

....

....

....

....

....

....

....

....

....

....

....

....

....

....

....

....

....

....

....

I am grateful to be pregnant with you because:

....
....
....
....
....
....
....
....
....
....
....
....
....
....
....
....
....
....
....
....
....
....
....
....

Some names I am considering for you:

....

....

....

....

....

....

....

....

....

....

....

....

....

....

....

....

....

....

....

....

....

....

....

....

....

Other notes to my growing baby:

....

....

....

....

....

....

....

....

....

....

....

....

....

....

....

....

....

....

....

....

....

....

....

....

....

....

Practice Exercises

START TRACKING THE GOOD

We hear a lot about what makes parenting difficult because it's often easier for people to air grievances than to share what is wonderful. This week, ask your friends and family with kids what they love most about being parents. Let their answers inform your vision for motherhood.

CREATE A VISION BOARD

- Choose a "feeling" word or intention that you want to center in your motherhood journey. (Some examples: sacred, beauty, grounded, strong, truth, power, etc.)

- Grab a stack of magazines and cut out any photos that resonate with you, demonstrate that word, or just inspire a feeling of warmth and support.

- Create a vision board from these images on a piece of cardstock or by gluing them to canvas.

- Remember that done is better than perfect: it's wonderful to get creative and fancy, but scotch tape and simple photos are great too.

- Put the board up somewhere you'll see a lot (such as the room you plan to feed/rock the baby to sleep in.)

First Trimester Affirmations

My baby and my body know exactly what to do

I accept and love my changing body

I am gentle with myself as I feel emotions rise and fall

I have everything I need to be the exact mother I want to be

I can handle things as they come and don't need to see the whole future

I know that I was built for this

I trust my body and my baby

The Second Trimester

The second trimester of pregnancy often brings some physical relief and might even find you with more emotional space to consider the future. Feeling baby's first kicks, your expanding waistline, and the awareness that you're literally carrying multiple hearts at once make this time rich with change, emotion, and wonder. There's also a realization that you're experiencing the same things your own mother, her mother, and all the birthing people who came before you have felt - a connection to yesterday, tomorrow, and the magic of life itself.

As you step into this charged place, allow the prompts on the following pages to guide you. Consider how this time is forging a new connection to your own mother, your growing baby, and an expansion of your inner knowing. Allow the questions to guide, resource, and awaken you to this new beautiful place.

You are growing into a stronger, more beautiful, and more deeply rooted human every day, dear one.

Second Trimester Reflections

WEEK

Symptoms I am feeling:..
....
....
....
....
....
....
....
....

WEEK

Symptoms I am feeling:..
....
....
....
....
....
....
....
....

WEEK

Symptoms I am feeling:..
....
....
....
....
....
....

Things I am craving: ....

....

....

....

....

....

....

....

Things that have surprised me about pregnancy: ....

....

....

....

....

....

....

What I am grateful for: ....

....

....

....

....

....

WEEK

I'm grateful to my body because: ....
....
....
....
....
....
....
....

WEEK

I'm grateful to my body because: ....
....
....
....
....
....
....
....

WEEK

I'm grateful to my body because: ....
....
....
....
....
....
....

Some mothers/parents that inspire me (alive or not, fictional or real, your own parents or parents of friends, etc.): ....

....

....

....

....

....

....

Qualities they possess (calm, trusting, communicative, fun, creative, etc.):

....

....

....

....

....

....

....

Qualities that will make me a good mother (list those you already possess and those you are growing): ....

....

....

....

....

....

Why I think my partner will make a good parent: ....
....
....
....
....
....
....
....

Resources, people, or activities I am finding energizing: ....
....
....
....
....
....
....
....

Where I can be more gentle with myself:...
....
....
....
....
....
....

Things I love about being pregnant:

....
....
....
....
....
....
....

Things I don't love about being pregnant:

....
....
....
....
....
....
....

Things I'm looking forward to eating/doing again after pregnancy:

....
....
....
....
....
....

I want more of these things (people, activities, feelings, etc.):

....
....
....
....
....
....
....
....
....
....
....
....
....
....
....
....
....
....
....
....
....
....
....
....

I want less of these things: (people, activities, feelings, etc.):

....

....

....

....

....

....

....

....

....

....

....

....

....

....

....

....

....

....

....

....

....

....

....

WEEK _How I am taking care of my mind, body, and spirit at this stage in pregnancy (doctor's visits, counseling, movement, nutrition, mindfulness, etc.):_ ....

....

....

....

....

....

....

WEEK _How I'm caring for my mind, body, & spirit:_ ....

....

....

....

....

....

....

....

WEEK _How I'm caring for my mind, body, & spirit:_ ....

....

....

....

....

....

....

WEEK _____

How I'm caring for my mind, body, & spirit: ....
....
....
....
....
....
....

WEEK _____

How I'm caring for my mind, body, & spirit: ....
....
....
....
....
....
....

WEEK _____

How I'm caring for my mind, body, & spirit: ....
....
....
....
....
....

How I will nurture my relationship

What do I imagine will be the biggest challenges to my relationship in early parenthood? How can I plan for these and arrange support, communication, and tools? (Some things to consider: sharing childcare, housework, finances, returning to work, sleep deprivation, time with friends, time alone, etc.):

....

....

....

....

....

....

....

....

....

....

....

....

....

....

....

....

....

....

....

....

....

How can I talk to my partner about these things in order to set our relationship up for success?

Write to Mom

What I want to share with you about this part of pregnancy:

....

....

....

....

....

....

....

....

....

....

....

....

....

....

....

....

....

....

....

....

....

....

....

How I am taking care of myself the way you would have (cooking or ordering a nourishing meal, physically resting and re-charging, gifting myself a cozy blanket or beautiful article of clothing, etc.):

....

....

....

....

....

....

....

....

....

....

....

....

....

....

....

....

....

....

....

....

....

....

....

....

Things I am currently struggling with that I wish I could share with you:

....
....
....
....
....
....
....
....
....
....
....
....
....
....
....
....
....
....
....
....
....
....
....
....

What I think you would say about these challenges:

Messages to Mom: ....
....
....
....
....
....
....
....
....
....
....
....
....
....
....
....
....
....
....
....
....
....
....
....
....
....
....
....
....

Write to Baby

WEEK .... YOU ARE CURRENTLY THE SIZE OF ....

Some memorable moments from this week: ....
....
....
....
....
....
....

WEEK .... YOU ARE CURRENTLY THE SIZE OF ....

Some memorable moments from this week: ....
....
....
....
....
....

WEEK .... YOU ARE CURRENTLY THE SIZE OF ....

Some memorable moments from this week: ....
....
....
....
....
....
....

I am grateful to be pregnant with you because:

....

....

....

....

....

....

....

....

....

....

....

....

....

....

....

....

....

....

....

....

....

....

....

....

....

....

The values I want to demonstrate for you through the way I am treating my pregnant self (compassion, love, patience, etc.):

....
....
....
....
....
....
....
....
....
....
....
....
....
....
....
....
....
....
....
....
....
....
....
....

Some things I hope you experience in life: ....

....

....

....

....

....

....

....

....

....

....

....

....

....

....

....

....

....

....

....

....

....

....

....

....

....

....

Why I am looking forward to meeting you: ....
....
....
....
....
....
....
....
....
....
....
....
....
....
....
....
....
....
....
....
....
....
....
....
....

Five things I want to teach you: ....

....

....

....

....

....

....

....

....

....

....

....

....

....

....

....

....

....

....

....

....

....

....

....

....

....

....

....

The most true and beautiful world I can imagine for you is:

Other notes to my growing baby:

....

....

....

....

....

....

....

....

....

....

....

....

....

....

....

....

....

....

....

....

....

....

....

....

....

Practice Exercises

ASK FOR A "MOTHER'S SHOWER"

At this point in your pregnancy you are likely planning a baby shower (or having one planned for you.) These events can invite lots of beautiful attention onto your baby, providing a chance for friends and family to celebrate and shower this new life. Welcoming your new baby is really special, but it's just as important (if not more) to incorporate aspects into your shower that also center you, the one embarking on the sacred new journey of motherhood.

Consider asking whomever is planning your shower to include a few exercises that mark this special transition, such as:

- Holding a birth story circle, where each mother present shares a positive birth story to give you hope, and those without kids share why they know you will be a great mom.

- Incorporating the memory of your own mother somehow (with a framed photo, an honorary chair, an altar, a spoken prayer, a candle, etc.)

- Creating a birth necklace of support. First, the shower guests gather in a circle where someone has brought a bag of beads or small objects to be strung onto a necklace. Have each woman choose an object, then speak a blessing for your birth journey and string the object onto a strand. Repeat with every person present. Bring this blessing strand with you into birth, remembering the strength and words infused within it.

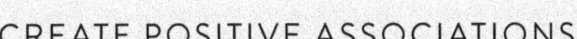

CREATE POSITIVE ASSOCIATIONS

Light a scented candle, burn a stick of incense, or lather on a body lotion that you enjoy. As the scent fills your senses, close your eyes and do some deep breaths, focusing on the way it feels for your belly to expand and relax. Do this for three minutes a day, and simply observe your breathing, notice the thoughts coming up, and allow this calm feeling to integrate with the soothing smell you've chosen. Allow an association to arise, and incorporate this smell into your birth plans and the early days of postpartum.

Second Trimester Affirmations

My baby and my body know exactly what to do

It is safe to enjoy pregnancy

My mind is relaxed, my heart is open, and I am supported on this journey

I know that my baby is safe

I trust my care team and my own ability to make decisions

My partner and I are the perfect parents for this baby

Love, peace, and protection surround my baby and me

The Third Trimester

Arriving in the third trimester of pregnancy can feel like being caught between two worlds.

There's your old existence of independence, alone time, and familiar ways of navigating life, and then there's the new world you're entering: the landscape of mother, nurturer, and a deeper vulnerability than you've ever experienced. The tiny kicks interrupting your dreams remind you that this child will soon be earth side, and that life as you know it is about to greatly change. This tectonic shifting can make you feel "all the things."

It's helpful at this point in your pregnancy to recognize the many ways you've been prepared for this. How even if you didn't know it at the time, your maternal instinct has been informed, nurtured, and influenced since the beginning - most notably by your own mother. However long she's been gone from the earth, her foundational love percolates the very soil your own mothering journey is taking root in. As you recognize the foundation resting beneath you, allow the prompts on the following pages to add grounding, confidence, and anchor you into this final stretch.

You are rising into motherhood rooted in love, guidance, and the power of so many women who have come before you. You were made for this, dear mama.

Third Trimester Reflections

WEEK ....

Symptoms I am feeling:..

....

....

....

....

....

....

WEEK ....

Symptoms I am feeling:..

....

....

....

....

....

....

WEEK ....

Symptoms I am feeling:..

....

....

....

....

....

Things that I am craving: ....

....

....

....

....

....

....

....

Things that are making me feel nourished (books, TV shows, foods, practices):

....

....

....

....

....

....

....

Friends and family that make me feel safe and supported: ....

....

....

....

....

....

....

WEEK

I am grateful to my body because: ....
....
....
....
....
....
....
....
....

WEEK

I am grateful to my body because: ....
....
....
....
....
....
....
....
....

WEEK

I am grateful to my body because: ....
....
....
....
....
....
....

What kind of mother I want to be (fun, stable, grounded, creative, etc.):

....

....

....

....

....

....

....

....

Where I currently experience those feelings (activities, people, media, etc.):

....

....

....

....

....

....

....

....

Ways I can incorporate these activities into my journey as a mother:

....

....

....

....

....

....

....

Practices I am doing to remember this pregnancy journey is sacred (prayer, meditation, writing here, etc.):

....

....

....

....

....

....

....

....

....

....

....

....

....

....

....

....

....

....

....

....

....

....

....

....

....

Things that make me feel drained (people, situations, tasks, activities):

....

....

....

....

....

....

....

....

How I can create boundaries to protect my time and self from things that make me feel drained (outsource a task that's been overwhelming, avoid a type of situation or certain media, ask for help with something related to the things listed above, etc.):

....

....

....

....

....

....

....

....

People I feel safe asking for help: ....

....

....

....

....

New mom and parent groups I have found locally (and virtually) that can offer me support after giving birth: ....
....
....
....
....
....
....
....
....
....
....
....
....
....
....
....
....
....
....
....
....
....
....
....
....

What pregnancy has taught me: ....

....

....

....

....

....

....

....

....

....

....

....

....

....

....

....

....

....

....

....

....

....

....

....

Things I am doing to feel prepared for birth (classes, preparing the home, yoga, breathwork, etc.):

....

....

....

....

....

....

....

Something I can make/find/create that will serve as a talisman (object of magic, strength, and stability) during early motherhood:

....

....

....

....

....

....

Where I can be more gentle with myself: ....

....

....

....

....

....

....

....

Write Your Birth Vision

*Different from a birth plan, a birth vision consists of the intentional **feelings** you envision in your birth story regardless of the exact sequence of events. (Examples: Powerful, grounded, autonomous, supported, loved, heard, held, strong, present, intentional, beautiful, etc.) After identifying and journaling the vision you have for your birth, take some time to close your eyes and actually imagine how this day would feel. As your pregnancy progresses, conjure your birth vision frequently; you are willing it into being while detaching from birth going exactly as planned.*

Write to Mom

The reasons I am grateful for the example you set for me as a mom:

....

....

....

....

....

....

....

....

....

....

....

....

....

....

....

....

....

....

....

....

....

....

....

The things I wish you could reassure me about: ....

....

....

....

....

....

....

....

....

....

....

....

....

....

....

....

....

....

....

....

....

....

The advice I think you would give me about childbirth:

....

....

....

....

....

....

....

....

....

....

....

....

....

....

....

....

....

....

....

....

....

....

....

....

....

....

The ways I am inviting you into my birth (meaningful object, affirmation, photo, etc.):

Messages to Mom: ....

....

....

....

....

....

....

....

....

....

....

....

....

....

....

....

....

....

....

....

....

....

....

....

....

....

....

....

Write to Baby

WEEK .... YOU ARE CURRENTLY THE SIZE OF ....

Some memorable moments from this week: ....

....

....

....

....

....

WEEK .... YOU ARE CURRENTLY THE SIZE OF ....

Some memorable moments from this week: ....

....

....

....

....

....

WEEK .... YOU ARE CURRENTLY THE SIZE OF ....

Some memorable moments from this week: ....

....

....

....

....

....

....

The dreams I have for our parent/child relationship:

Some places I look forward to introducing you to:

....

....

....

....

....

....

....

....

....

....

....

....

....

....

....

....

....

....

....

....

....

....

....

....

....

....

....

....

I am grateful for you because: ....

....

....

....

....

....

....

....

....

....

....

....

....

....

....

....

....

....

....

....

....

....

....

....

....

I look forward to meeting you because: ....

....

....

....

....

....

....

....

....

....

....

....

....

....

....

....

....

....

....

....

....

....

....

....

....

....

Other notes to my growing baby: ....

....

....

....

....

....

....

....

....

....

....

....

....

....

....

....

....

....

....

....

....

....

....

....

....

....

....

Practice Exercises

PLAN A PREGNANCY DATE

Treat yourself to a day of doing things that fill you with wonder, creativity, or that just sound plain fun. Maybe this looks like taking yourself out for an ice cream sundae, browsing a craft store for some creative supplies, buying yourself a beautiful (and comfortable) maternity outfit, or going to your favorite natural foods store to smell the variety of lotions, oils, and creams they carry (that are also good for your body and baby.) Allow yourself to meander, become side-tracked, and go home and nap at the end if you'd like. Taking yourself on a pregnancy date is the gift you give yourself.

REMEMBER YOUR POWER

Bring to mind some brave things that you've done or overcome in the past: These can be as big as going to a new country, or as seemingly small as telling someone an uncomfortable truth. Make a list of these courageous things and allow them to remind you that you are up to the work of giving birth and being a mother.

....
....
....
....
....
....
....
....
....
....
....
....
....
....

Third Trimester Affirmations:

My bump is the exact right size for my baby

My baby and my body know exactly what to do

I am willing to let go of old identities and make way for the person I am now becoming

I am powerful, brave, and strong

My baby will find the perfect position for birth

I know that my mom is surrounding us with love, protection, and guidance

Birth Affirmations

Use the following birth affirmations to prepare, empower, and ground you during your birth experience. Feel free to personalize them or create your own; focus on those that feel particularly calming, hopeful, and bring strength.

An idea: write an affirmation on a piece of cardstock each day, then take some time to color the words in or add a drawing. This is a great practice for just before bed or right when you wake. When it comes time to give birth, put these cards up where you can see them as you labor or in your birth room. It can also be helpful to record yourself saying the affirmations, listen to the recorded track often, and then play it during labor or in preparation for birth. Allow these words to trigger peace, calm, and the positive associations you created while making them.

My birthing body is magic

Birth is beautiful

Each surge brings my baby closer to me

My baby and my body know exactly what to do

However our birth happens is the right way for baby and me

I know that birth is safe

I know that my baby is safe

The surges come from my body so they cannot be stronger than me

I trust my care team and my own ability to make decisions

I am supported by my partner, my care team, and my Higher Power

My body was made to give birth

My mom and my ancestors are surrounding and supporting me

I am powerful, brave, and strong

I am enrobed in the protection of millions of mothers who have gone before me

My baby has a Higher Power and I am not it

It is safe to let go

I can do anything for sixty seconds

My baby and I are surrounded by God's love and guidance

I am exactly who my baby needs

MY BABY'S

Arrival

Use the following pages to record important circumstances and notes involving the birth of your new baby. Congratulations, mama — you did it!

Baby's Arrival

Full name: ....
....

Birth date: ....

Time: .... Weight: .... Length: ....

Place of birth: ....
....

Doctor/midwife/doula's names:
....
....
....
....

Others present:

....

....

....

....

Notable circumstances in the world (weather, news stories, cultural events, etc.):

....

....

....

....

First words spoken:

....

....

....

....

Music/sounds/smells I remember:

....

....

....

....

How my partner reacted: ....

....

....

....

What I'll remember most:

The Fourth Trimester

The first few months after your baby is born (sometimes called the fourth trimester) might be the most shocking part of motherhood. The moment of birth catapults you into a new world: one containing an adorable being entirely dependent on you, a body that just did something incredible (but that now feels incredibly foreign) and an identity that, like your old clothes, just doesn't fit the same.

And just as you are patient with your new baby's needs, investigating their cries with curiosity and not expecting them to know how to do most things, allow the same space for yourself. Commit to recognizing what's necessary for you to feel nourished, supported, and reassured in this new part of life. Try to approach your new motherhood difficulties not with judgment, but with curiosity and compassion. It's okay to feel shaky, uncertain, and lost. You're not doing any of this wrong, dear one.

Use the prompts on the following pages to reflect and open your heart, tend to your spirit, and love on yourself the way your own mother would if she were here. Recognize that in being gentle with your newborn mama self you are by proxy becoming a better mother, partner, and human in the world. It serves everyone for you to value the business of self-nourishment.

Fourth Trimester Reflections

(**WEEK**)

Things I am grateful to my body for: ....

....

....

....

....

....

....

(**WEEK**)

Things I am grateful to my body for: ....

....

....

....

....

....

....

(**WEEK**)

Things I am grateful to my body for: ....

....

....

....

....

....

My postpartum symptoms include: ....
....
....
....
....
....
....
....

Some things I love about this time: ....
....
....
....
....
....
....
....

Some things I am struggling with: ....
....
....
....
....
....

The places I feel most depleted: ....
....
....
....
....
....
....
....

How I could resource help in those places (laundry service, asking friend to pick up coffee, asking partner to take over a night time feeding, etc.):
....
....
....
....
....
....

The people who I can ask for help/support right now are: ....
....
....
....
....
....
....

Ways I am taking care of my mental health (making/keeping therapy appointments, reaching out for support, listening to what my body needs, eating foods that feel good, etc.):

The things that are nourishing me right now: ....

....

....

....

....

....

....

....

....

....

....

....

....

....

....

....

....

....

....

....

....

....

Things I am grateful to my partner for:...

....

....

....

....

....

....

....

Places I need more support from my partner: ....

....

....

....

....

....

....

....

The most surprising thing about this time:...

....

....

....

....

....

....

....

Five resources to reach for when I'm struggling (counseling service, postpartum support group, mother's support group, attending a group around another personal interest, etc.)

....

....

....

....

....

....

....

....

....

....

....

....

....

....

....

....

....

....

....

....

....

....

Five ways I am already doing a great job as a mother (Are you getting to know your baby's different needs? Getting a hang of the carseat? Soothing baby to sleep like only you can do? Nothing is too small to list here!)

Write down your birth story

Here you can record the details you want to remember about your baby's birth. Consider things like the days leading up to labor, the way you felt, what you noticed about the hospital room or your birth team, your first thoughts after delivery, who was present, how you felt as you recovered, etc.

....

....

....

....

....

....

....

....

....

....

....

....

....

....

....

....

....

....

....

....

....

....

Write to Mom

The advice I think you would give me about these early days:

....
....
....
....
....
....
....
....
....
....
....
....
....
....
....
....
....
....
....
....
....
....
....
....

The things I wish you could reassure me about: ....

....

....

....

....

....

....

....

....

....

....

....

....

....

....

....

....

....

....

....

....

....

....

Some things I wonder if you felt too: ....

....

....

....

....

....

....

....

....

....

....

....

....

....

....

....

....

....

....

....

....

....

....

....

....

....

....

Ways I will make sure that my child knows you (sharing stories about mom on special milestones, donating in your name to a cause you cared about, doing something kind for another that we would have done for you, passing along values that you instilled in me, etc.):

....

....

....

....

....

....

....

....

....

....

....

....

....

....

....

....

....

....

....

....

....

....

....

....

Messages to Mom:

Write to Baby

The things I already love about you: ....

....

....

....

....

....

....

....

....

....

....

....

....

....

....

....

....

....

....

....

....

....

....

....

....

....

Some things you do that make me smile:

My intention(s) for this first year of your life (to be present, open, compassionate, calm, trusting, etc.):

....

....

....

....

....

....

....

....

....

....

....

....

....

....

....

....

....

....

....

....

....

....

....

....

....

A quality of my mom's that I hope to demonstrate for you:

....

....

....

....

....

....

....

....

....

....

....

....

....

....

....

....

....

....

....

....

....

....

....

....

Why I'm grateful to be your mom:

Other notes to my baby: ....
....
....
....
....
....
....
....
....
....
....
....
....
....
....
....
....
....
....
....
....
....
....
....
....
....
....
....

Practice Exercises

ASK FOR SUPPORT

If you're struggling in these early days, asking for help is massively important. It might be helpful to send a text like this to a few close friends and family: "Hi, I am just checking in. These first weeks have been hard and I would love to ask for your support by (insert an idea here.)" It could be having someone over to help with tasks around the house, asking someone to run an errand for you, or simply asking a friend to check in with you via text so that you feel less alone. People often want to help but don't know how; while you are still figuring out what kind of support you need, simply sending up a flare of connection can be helpful.

ACCESS YOUR INNER ANCHOR

Recall a moment from your childhood where you felt uncon-ditionally loved and supported (by your own mom or another.) Close your eyes and imagine the space you were in, what smells there might have been, the texture of the objects in the room, etc. Allow yourself to feel that safety, support, and love. After you've conjured this memory, breathe with it as long as you feel called, and then open your eyes. Put it in your back pocket as a touchstone for moments you need that stability, safety, and love. If you feel so moved, write about this vision below.

Fourth Trimester Affirmations

I am surrounded by my mother's love, protection, and guidance

I know that my baby is safe

I am getting to know my baby better every day

It is safe to disappoint people as I embrace this new version of myself

The right people will love me exactly as I am

It is safe to ask for help

My mental, spiritual, and physical health are valuable

Taking care of myself is loving to everyone around me

I am gentle with myself as I learn how to mother

My best is always good enough and I am doing my best

I know that everything changes and no one phase will last forever

I am a good mother

I am the best mother for this baby

I am doing an amazing job

I am always guided, held, and supported on this path

AFTERWORD:

An Ode to Magic, Mystery, and Mothers

As my second pregnancy came to a close, my daughter was *way* overdue and I was feeling pressure to be induced.

Though we both looked healthy on the monitors, the doctors kept warning of stillbirth, placental failure, and all of the medical reasons to *just get her out*. Since my induction with my first had taken three days and been quite traumatic, I continued to resist their suggestions.

Most of my resolve came from a foggy memory of my own mom's birth stories: my brother was two weeks overdue and I was three weeks late. Since I'd carried late with my first (forty two weeks and three days) I reasoned that women in our family must have longer gestations, and kept declining the induction — but on the inside I was quaking.

What if something DOES go wrong? How will I ever forgive myself? Am I harming my baby?

I prayed a lot, feeling at once powerless and also TOO powerful, with the choice to induce always mine and constantly presented. I kept asking my mom for help, all the while cursing that, again, she's not here to *actually* ask.

A darkness set in.

As my daughter's due date grew further away, I reluctantly agreed to an induction on the following Monday. A few days beforehand one of my close friends dropped by; she knew I was struggling and said she'd brought me a healing stone from her house.

"Not that you need healing necessarily, but I was moved to bring it," she said, holding up a small glittering rock. "It's called peacock stone."

I thanked her and tucked the stone into my bra above my heart — I was open to all bits of help, and this little stone (and visit from a friend) lifted my spirits.

Later that day, feeling moved to collect more talismans, I searched high and low for a bracelet I wanted to wear during birth. It had disappeared months earlier, and a part of me had become convinced I wouldn't go into labor until I found it.

When again I came up empty handed, I decided that in lieu of the bracelet, I'd find something of my mom's to wear. I returned to the jewelry case and my eyes settled on something I hadn't noticed during any of my previous searches...a bracelet.

A bracelet of my mom's that I'd kept because of the colors, sparkle, and beauty, but in a shape I'd never before noticed...

A peacock.

I immediately slid it on my wrist and felt goosebumps all over.

I decided to look up the significance of peacocks, and found that among other things, they represent:

Guidance
Holiness
Watchfulness
Protection

I felt my whole being exhale.

That night I went to sleep with a newfound feeling of acceptance that my baby would arrive when she was ready. I felt comfort knowing that we had the protection, guidance, and watchfulness of Great Forces — including my mom.

"My baby has a Higher Power and I am not it," I had written on my mirror weeks earlier — but for the first time, I truly believed it.

Early the next morning, I woke up to contractions that were far more painful than the false starts I'd been experiencing for weeks. My daughter Mirabel arrived so quickly I almost gave birth in our hallway — a labor so swift she emerged mere moments after arriving at the hospital.

Both of us were perfectly healthy when she was born "late" at forty two weeks and four days.

Also known as the exact right timing.

My plump little peacock.

• • •

At the time of writing, my mom has been gone from this earth for nearly nine years. I long for her voice, her sense of humor, and the way her mere presence on the planet could reassure me like nothing else has since. I will always miss her.

But I recount this story because within it I see that great forces — and reassuring peacock moments — abound for all of us. I feel how my mother's impact is still grounding me today — and shaping me into the same force for my own children.

Your mom's ever-present love is doing the same for you.

Today, as your grief and love mix together and build a foundation for this new life, I ask you to join me in sending up a thank you to our mommas in the stars.

May they continue to shine on, down, and through us.

May we never stop looking for their magic . . . or remembering our own.

• • •

I hope that this journal has reminded you of a few things.

I hope it has guided you toward your own maternal instincts, cultivated a sense of beauty and self-love, and allowed you to weave a connection between your baby, your mom, and your own sacred path. The exercises and prompts sprang from what I most needed during my pregnancies, and I truly hope that they nourished you. I'm honored to have been a small part of your sacred journey into motherhood. Please remember you are never alone on this path.

Wishing you the most beautiful motherhood, dear reader.

I know *your mom would be **so** proud of you.*

With Love,
Melissa Pennel

PREGNANCY & POSTPARTUM
MENTAL HEALTH RESOURCES

Mental health is always important, but the pregnancy/postpartum period is an especially tender time. There is no shame in accessing tools to support you on this journey. Use the below resources as a starting point to accessing support locally. You are not alone and there is help.

POSTPARTUM SUPPORT INTERNATIONAL
Website: Postpartum.net
Phone: 1-800-944-4773

SAMHSA (Substance Abuse and Mental Health Services Administration)
Website: SAMHSA.gov
Phone: 1-800-662-HELP (4357)

NAMI (National Alliance on Mental Illness)
Website: NAMI.org
Phone: 1-800-950-NAMI (6264)

NATIONAL SUICIDE PREVENTION LIFELINE
Website: suicidepreventionlifeline.org
Phone: 1-800-273-8255

For **non-crisis** ongoing virtual support (in a group composed of other motherless postpartum moms) join the "Motherless Mothers: Pregnancy & Postpartum Support" group on Facebook

About the Author

Melissa Pennel is a mother, life coach, and author. She believes in the healing power of words, that motherhood is sacred, and that everyone is a writer if given the right prompts.

Melissa lives in Northern California with her partner, children, and beloved cats.

Find more of Melissa's work at FollowYourFireCoaching.com.

This journal is in memory of her mother, deLise Rae Cline-Pennel.

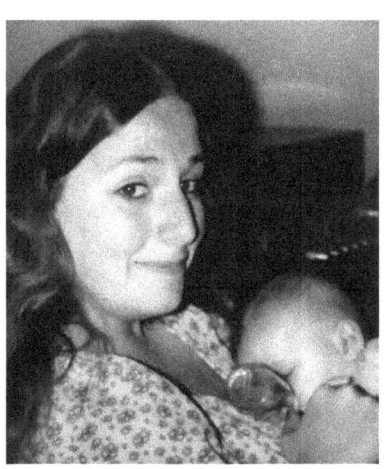 

www.ingramcontent.com/pod-product-compliance
Lightning Source LLC
Chambersburg PA
CBHW051629120626
46551CB00014B/1996